Letts

You think *you* have a long journey to school? Meet the Alien ⬚, aliens from the planet Dunk. They all entered a competition a⬚ ⬚ ⬚ ⬚ ⬚ to school on planet Earth, six thousand light years away! Lucky their space-mobile runs on recycled rubbish and can travel a hundred light years in a heartbeat!

Meet **Nok**, who finds football much easier than school, but tries all the same!

Twinx, who loves ribbons, dancing and her toy friend Mini T.

Bouncing **Pogo**, who just can't stand still!

Pogo's pet dog, the rather less lively **Zen**, who won't get out of bed for less than a Z cookie or two.

Zara P, zip zip zipping around on her scooter and making notes on everything she sees.

And **Zing**, who loves his music most of all, but thinks school is pretty cool too!

Now the Alien Club want to pass on everything they have learnt to you. All you have to do is work your way through these tests and not only will you be the cleverest Earthling around, you'll become a member of the Alien Club too! Out of this world!!!

THE **ALIEN CLUB**

English 9–10

Alison Head

Zip, zip, zip! I'm Zara P and I like to zip around on my scooter and make notes in my notebook. I've just learnt that most words that end in a vowel, end in e, but I have some in my notebook that end in a, i, o and u.

Never fear, ZP is here!

To turn these words into plurals, you can usually just add s, but with some words that end in o, you have to add es, and some can be spelt either way!

disc**os**   domin**oes**   mang**os** or mang**oes**

I'll just make a note of that…

Write down the plural of these words.

1 camera _____
2 halo _____
3 cuckoo _____
4 radio _____
5 hero _____
6 chapatti _____
7 tuba _____
8 zoo _____

9 area _____
10 echo _____
11 gnu _____
12 piano _____
13 emu _____
14 banana _____
15 tango _____

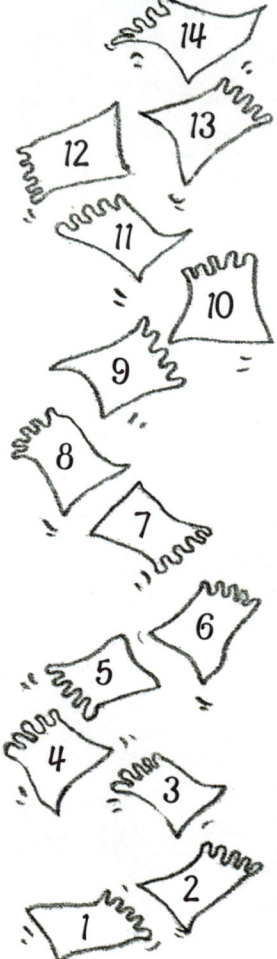

You're zippy! Have a scooter sticker for your certificate at the back of the book.

Colour in your score.

Hey there! I'm Zing. There's no need to stress about **plurals**, as long as you know the rules. Most words end **s** in the plural, but words that end **s**, **x**, **sh** or **ch** in the singular usually end **es** in the plural.

stars   boxes

Words which end in a consonant followed by **y**, end **ies**.

babies

Circle the planet showing the correct plural.

1 planeties   planets   planetes

2 foxs   foxies   foxes

3 shoes   shoeies   shoees

4 skys   skyes   skies

5 bushies   bushs   bushes

6 torches   torchs   torchies

7 lorrys   lorries   lorryes

8 beeis   bees   beees

9 ladys   ladyes   ladies

10 eyies   eyees   eyes

11 buses   busses   buss

12 puppys   puppies   puppyies

13 crateres   craters   crateries

14 studies   studys   studyes

15 friendes   friendies   friends

15
14
13
12
11
10
9
8
7
6
5
4
3
2
1

Colour in your score.

Prefixes

Hello! I'm Twinx and this is my toy friend Mini T. Did you know that all these words start with a **prefix**, and each prefix has a different meaning?

tele = over a distance   **tele**phone

bi = two   **bi**cycle

trans = across   **trans**port

auto = by itself   **auto**mobile

circum = around   **circum**ference

That should help me to work out what they mean and how to spell them. Hurray!

Choose the best prefix from the television to complete each word.

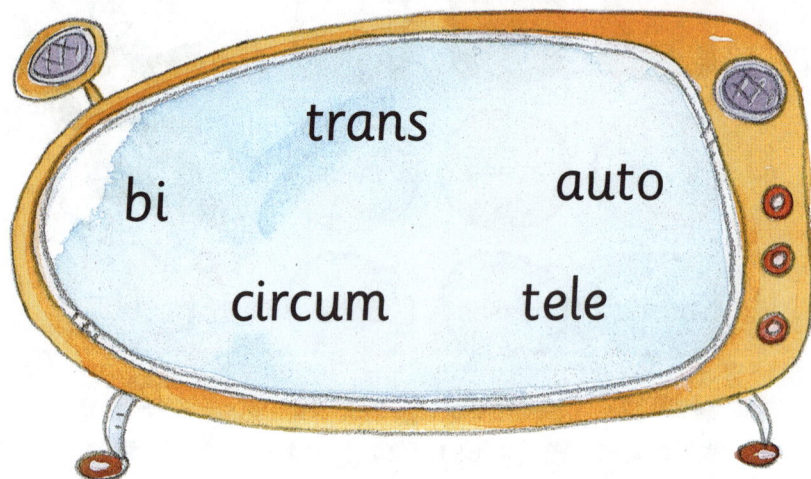

trans

bi

auto

circum

tele

1 _____focal

2 _____mit

3 _____stance

4 _____matic

5 _____biography

6 _____noculars

7 _____late

8 _____navigate

9 _____scope

10 _____nary

11 _____vision

12 _____vent

13 _____pilot

14 _____pathy

15 _____fer

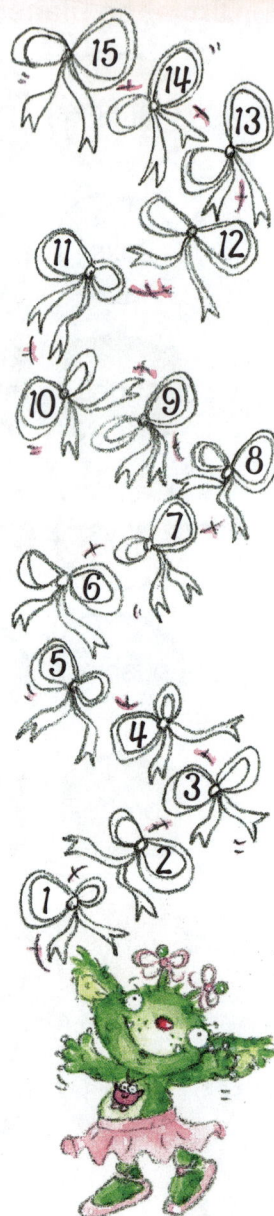

Hurray! Have a Mini T sticker for your certificate.

Colour in your score.

Synonyms

Hello. I'm Zen. Apart from eating my owner Pogo's Z cookies, I just like to sleep, doze, snooze, slumber… zzz.

These words are all **synonyms** – words that have similar meanings.

Using synonyms saves you having to use the same tired words all the time in your writing, making it much more interesting.

Just make sure you choose one with exactly the right meaning – some are more extreme than others.

Underline the more extreme word in each pair.

1. cross | furious
2. hilarious | amusing
3. hungry | starving
4. saturated | wet
5. cool | freezing
6. ancient | old
7. ecstatic | contented
8. warm | boiling
9. sprint | jog
10. hurl | toss
11. miserable | sad
12. dazzling | bright
13. loud | deafening
14. tired | exhausted
15. cracked | shattered

15 14 13 12 11 10 9 8 7 6 5 4 3 2 1

Good work! Have a Z cookie sticker for your certificate.

Colour in your score.

More prefixes

Err, what? I'm Nok, and apart from football, I find everything a bit confusing – especially **prefixes**! The prefixes ir, im and in often mean the same thing – not. They're really useful for making opposites.

accurate **in**accurate

You have to remember which words go with each prefix though. Words which start with r, usually have the ir prefix, but you just have to learn the others.

Circle the correctly spelt word in each pair.

1 inactive | iractive
2 irrational | imrational
3 imcredible | incredible
4 inregular | irregular
5 imconsiderate | inconsiderate
6 irreversible | inreversible
7 inpure | impure
8 imdirect | indirect
9 irreplaceable | ineplaceable
10 irrelevant | inrelevant
11 immature | inmature
12 inperfect | imperfect
13 irdecisive | indecisive
14 impersonal | inpersonal
15 inpolite | impolite

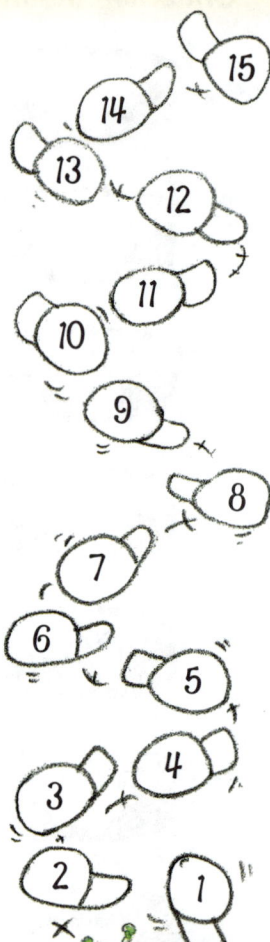

Goal! Have a football sticker.

Colour in your score.

Adverbs

Boing, boing, boing! I'm Pogo. When you're writing a story, really great character dialogue is just a bounce away if you team up verbs and **adverbs** to say how, as well as what, your characters are saying.

'Please find me a Z cookie!' pleaded Zen, **pitifully**.

Do you see how the verb pleaded and the adverb pitifully work together?

Think of some great adverbs to fill the gaps in these sentences.

1 'Come on, Mini T, let's dance,' giggled Twinx, _____.

2 'Check out my new trainers,' said Zing, _____.

3 'I'm dog tired!' yawned Zen, _____.

4 Pogo shouted _____, 'I love bouncing!'

5 'Tickets, please!' snapped the space-mobile driver, _____.

6 'He was offside!' complained Nok, _____.

7 'Look, there's planet Earth!' gasped Twinx, _____.

8 'Whee! Zip, zip, zip!' laughed Zara P, _____.

9 'Can we go shopping?' asked Twinx, _____.

10 'Turn up the music,' requested Zing, _____.

11 'What's that?' wondered Zara P, _____.

12 'Mmmm! Z cookies,' murmured Zen, _____.

13 'Shall we play in the crater?' suggested Twinx, _____.

14 'Hurry,' panted Zing, _____, 'the space-mobile is about to leave.'

15 'Err, what?' mumbled Nok, _____.

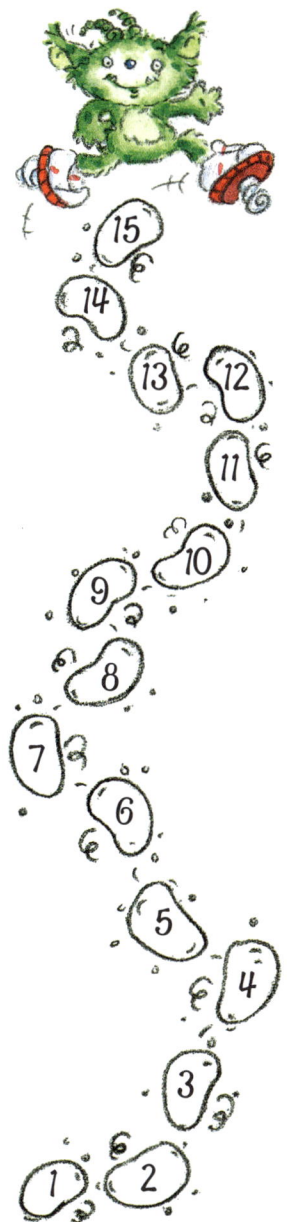

Put a spring in your step! Have a springy sticker.

Colour in your score.

Checking for mistakes

If I make a **mistake** on my jet scooter, I usually end up in the mud! Luckily, correcting the writing in my notebook is much easier.

You can improve your writing too, by proofreading it carefully for mistakes when you've finished. Look for spelling and punctuation mistakes, and check that all your sentences make sense.

Underline the mistakes in each of these sentences.

1 Remember not to be lait for the rocket launch.

2 Nok is filthy because he, has been playing football again.

3 Zing downloaded has more music.

4 The sunset was imcredible last night.

5 Zen was, asleep, so Pogo got out another Z cookie.

6 Twinx is practising her ballet

7 Nok has eaten four ice lollys today!

8 Pogo bounces all over the plaice.

9 my jet scooter needs a good clean.

10 Twinx playing is with Mini T.

11 Look how brite that star is!

12 the fleet of space ships has landed.

13 'Hella!' said Twinx.

14 Zing loves to cool look.

15 Zen is always sleeping

15
14
13 12 11
10
9
8 7
6
5
4
3 2
1

You're zippy! Have a scooter sticker.

Colour in your score.

Direct and reported speech

The referee said I was offside, but I say, 'Goal!'

When I told you what the referee said, without using his actual words, I was using **reported speech**.

Direct speech is where you quote a person's actual words, using proper speech punctuation, like me yelling, 'Goal!'

Direct speech is great, because it means characters in your stories can talk to each other, but using reported speech lets you show what someone says without them actually having to be in the story at that moment.

Work out whether these sentences are direct speech (D) or reported speech (R). Write your answers in the goals.

1 'Wait for me!' cried Zing.

2 'Can I play with you?' asked Twinx.

3 Zara P said she was going out.

4 'I'm off for a bounce!' laughed Pogo.

5 Zen told Pogo he was hungry.

6 The aliens all counted down from ten before the rocket took off.

7 Nok said, 'Have you seen my football boots?'

8 'Can I help you?' asked the alien shopkeeper.

9 The space-mobile mechanic explained that the fuel system was blocked.

10 Twinx complained that she was hungry.

11 'I don't understand!' wailed Nok.

12 'Never fear, Zara P is here!'

13 Pogo said he could see a comet.

14 'This music is so cool,' said Zing.

15 Nok said he was going outside to play.

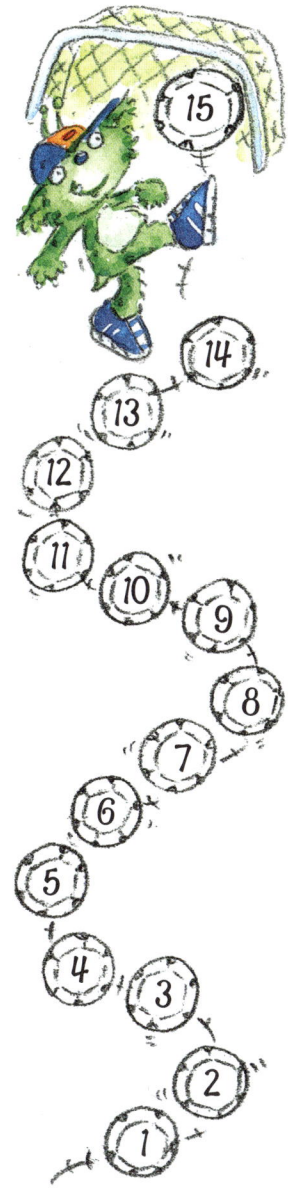

Goal! Have a football sticker.

Colour in your score.

Zip, zip, zip! I have loads of things in my bag. We use **nouns** to name things, and there are different types of nouns for different things…

Common nouns name people or things.

Abstract nouns name a feeling or idea.

alien   star   tiredness   love

Proper nouns name specific people or places, as well as the days of the week, months of the year, and things like the names of books and films. They all start with a capital letter.

Dunk   Pogo

Sort these nouns into the correct groups.

1 Earth
2 anger
3 knowledge
4 Friday
5 planet
6 confusion
7 crater
8 happiness
9 rocket
10 Zen
11 scooter
12 January
13 hatred
14 comet
15 Twinx

Common nouns

_____
_____
_____
_____
_____

Abstract nouns

_____
_____
_____
_____
_____

Proper nouns

_____
_____
_____
_____
_____

You're zippy! Have a scooter sticker.

Colour in your score.

Imperative verbs

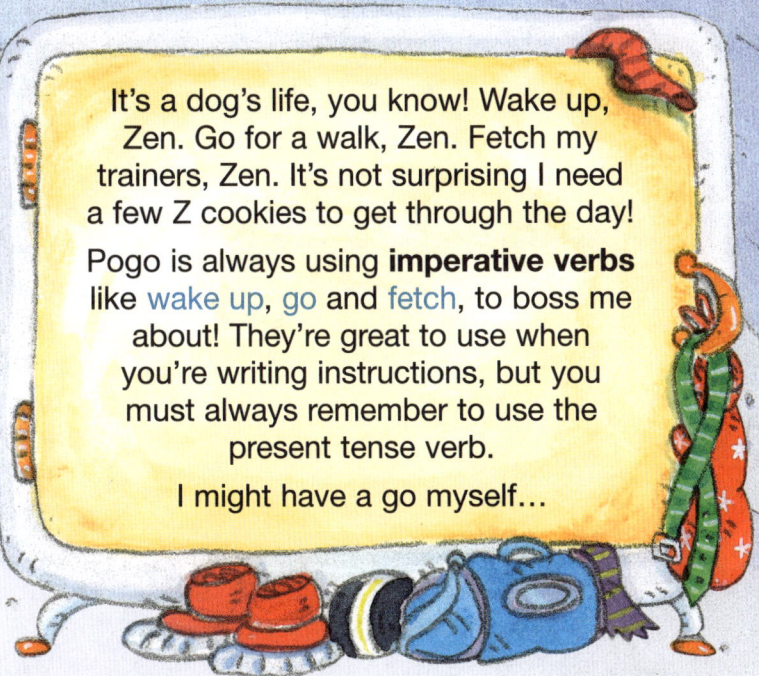

It's a dog's life, you know! Wake up, Zen. Go for a walk, Zen. Fetch my trainers, Zen. It's not surprising I need a few Z cookies to get through the day!

Pogo is always using **imperative verbs** like wake up, go and fetch, to boss me about! They're great to use when you're writing instructions, but you must always remember to use the present tense verb.

I might have a go myself...

Underline the imperative verbs in Zen's note to Pogo.

1 Locate your springy trainers.
2 Put them on.
3 Bounce down to the shop.
4 Choose the biggest box of Z cookies in the shop.
5 Take out your money.
6 Pay for the cookies.
7 Wait for your change.
8 Bring the cookies back home.
9 Find a very large bowl.
10 Fill it to the brim.
11 Place the bowl on the floor beside me.
12 Refill it when I've finished.
13 Clear up the crumbs on the floor.
14 Fetch me a cushion.
15 Leave me in peace, for a nap!

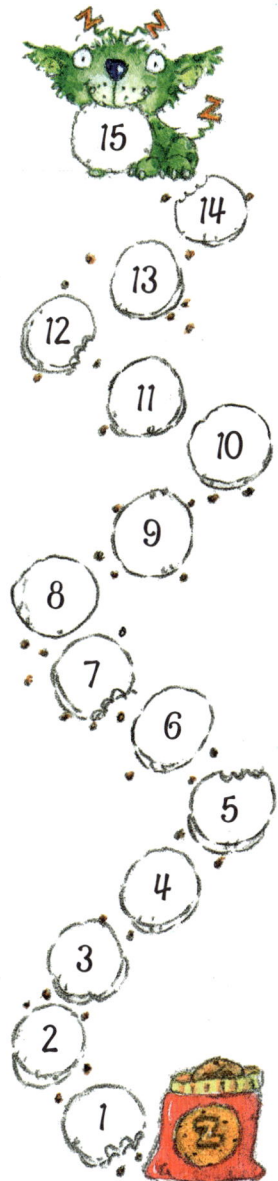

Good work! Have a Z cookie sticker.

Colour in your score.

Wow! English is so cool! You sometimes say things like 'Sammy is over the moon', but you don't mean that he is here on planet Dunk – you mean that he is really happy!

Phrases like that are called **idioms**. When you use them, you don't actually mean what you say, but most people know what they really mean, so they can help to bring your characters' dialogue to life.

Draw lines to match up the idioms with their meanings.

1 He's worth his salt.

2 I could eat a horse.

3 Let's paint the town red!

4 It's raining cats and dogs!

5 He opened a can of worms.

6 Don't put the cart before the horse.

7 He was born with a silver spoon in his mouth.

8 We're like chalk and cheese.

9 Put your thinking cap on!

10 Her head is in the clouds.

11 She's the apple of his eye.

12 I'm hopping mad!

13 Let's tie the knot.

14 You're pulling my leg!

15 I'm feeling under the weather.

A I'm really cross!

B Think carefully!

C You're teasing me!

D She's his favourite.

E Don't get things back to front.

F She's daydreaming.

G Let's get married.

H I'm not feeling well.

I Let's have a big celebration!

J He caused a lot of problems.

K It's raining very hard!

L He was born into a rich family.

M We're completely different.

N He's a really useful person.

O I'm very hungry.

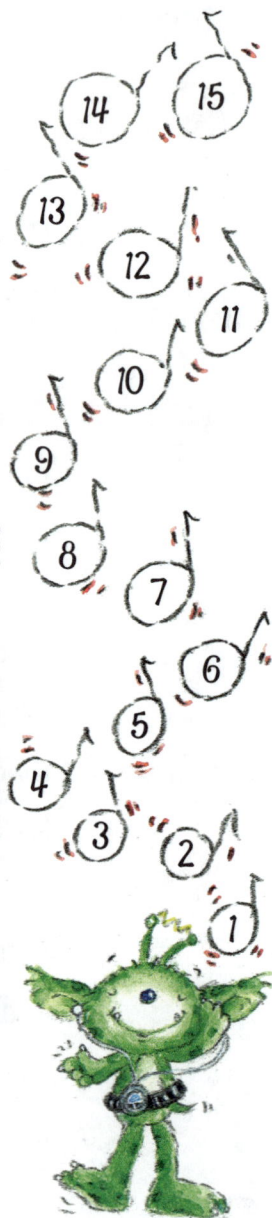

Easy! Have a musical sticker.

Colour in your score.

I'm playing a *grate* game with Mini T. Oops! Sorry, I should have said a *great* game, shouldn't I? Oh dear, Mini T, I do find **homophones** tricky. They are words that sound the same but are spelt differently and have different meanings. You have to be really careful to choose the right one when you're writing.

Circle the right homophone for each sentence.

1 The space-mobile turns **waste waist** into fuel.

2 Planet Dunk is closer to the **son sun** than planet Earth.

3 Nok went out to **buy by** some new trainers.

4 Twinx is not **allowed aloud** to stay up late tonight.

5 Zen **eight ate** a whole box of Z cookies.

6 Nok **threw through** his ball and it broke a window.

7 Zara P loves looking at the stars in the **night knight** sky.

8 Zing read Twinx a fairy **tail tale** at bedtime.

9 The aliens had to **weight wait** for the next space-mobile.

10 Twinx left her toys all over her bedroom **floor flaw**.

11 Nok fetched a Z cookie **for four** Zen.

12 Twinx brought a teddy **bare bear** back from planet Earth.

13 The space-mobile driver slammed on the **brakes breaks**.

14 Zing tried feeding **bread bred** and butter to Zen.

15 Zara P **kneads needs** more fuel for her jet scooter.

Hurray! Have a Mini T sticker.

Colour in your score.

Boing, boing, boing! I'm always bounc**ing** and hopp**ing** about! To describe what people are doing right now, you need to add **ing** to the verb.

You can usually just add **ing** without changing the spelling of the verb, but if it ends in **e**, you take off the final **e** first…

bounce   bounc**ing**

…and if it has a short vowel sound before the final consonant, you double the final letter.

hop   hopp**ing**

Complete these word sums by adding ing to the verbs. Write the new words in the boxes.

1 take + ing =

2 go + ing =

3 fly + ing =

4 run + ing =

5 write + ing =

6 travel + ing =

7 leave + ing =

8 eat + ing =

9 dream + ing =

10 believe + ing =

11 win + ing =

12 read + ing =

13 sit + ing =

14 get + ing =

15 live + ing=

Put a spring in your step! Have a springy sticker.

Colour in your score.

TEST 14 Antonyms

My dancing used to be dreadful, but now it's brilliant! Words like dreadful and brilliant, with opposite meanings, are called **antonyms**. They help us to compare and contrast things in our writing.

Some words have one antonym.

dead   alive

Some words have several antonyms.

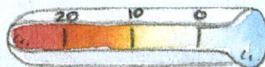

hot   cool   cold   freezing

Now come on, Mini T, let's dance!

Complete the crossword grid by thinking of antonyms for each word.

Across		Down	
1 sad	5 heavy	8 float	12 tied
2 behave	6 wide	9 awake	13 dirty
3 found	7 go	10 slow	14 thin
4 thaw		11 above	15 hot

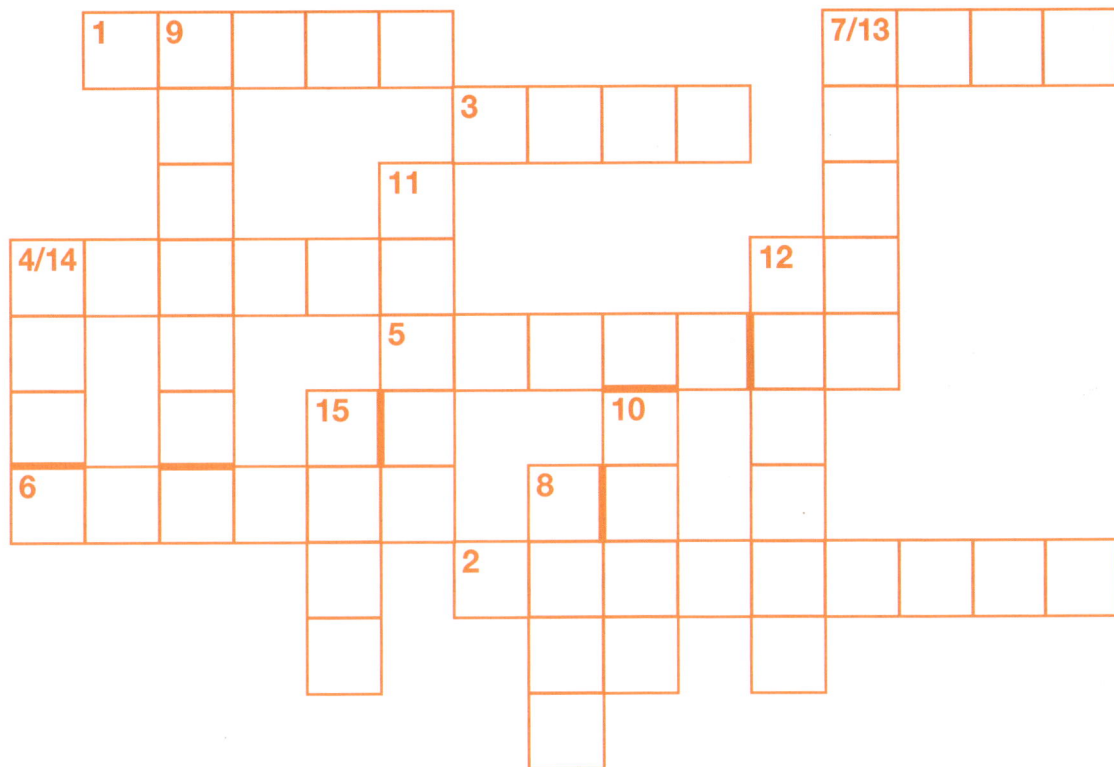

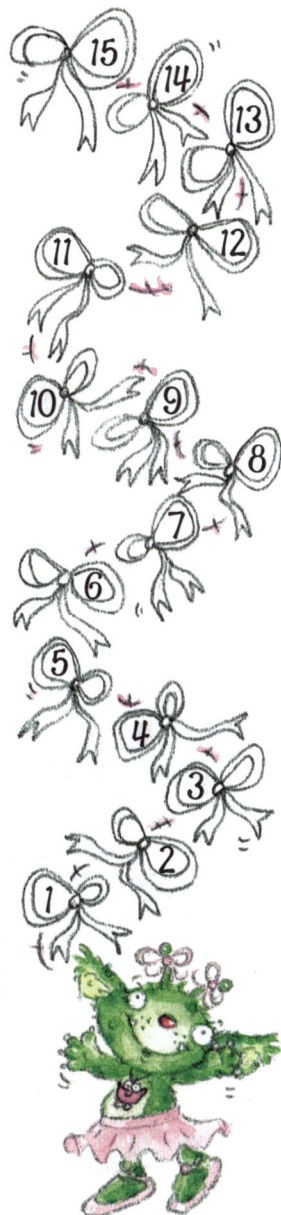

 Hurray! Have a Mini T sticker.

Colour in your score.

Onomatopoeia

Munch, chomp, gobble, slurp, crunch! These Z cookies sound as great as they taste! Words like gobble and crunch are **onomatopoeias**. That means that when you say them out loud, they sound like the noises they describe.

Onomatopoeias are really useful for bringing your writing to life.

Write down three onomatopoeias for each of these sounds.

a raindrop hitting the ground

1 _____
2 _____
3 _____

a window breaking

4 _____
5 _____
6 _____

a firework

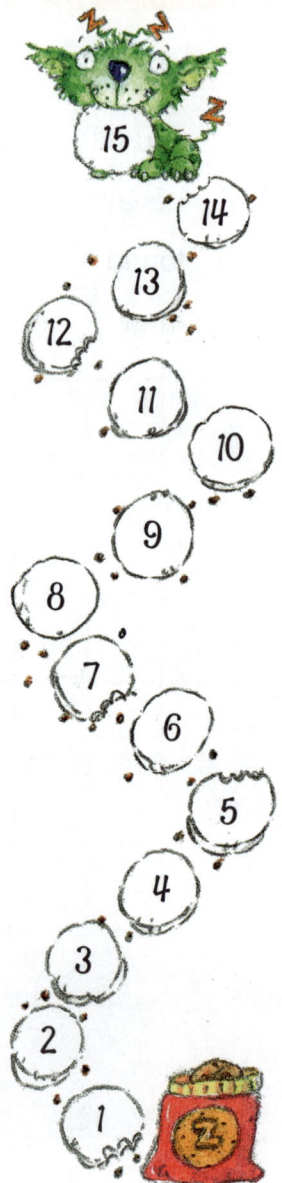

7 _____
8 _____
9 _____

a bird noise

10 _____
11 _____
12 _____

a baby crying

13 _____
14 _____
15 _____

15 14 13 12 11 10 9 8 7 6 5 4 3 2 1

Good work! Have a Z cookie sticker.

Colour in your score.

Spoken and written English

Wow! **Spoken English** is totally different from **written English**.

When you speak, you don't always use complete sentences and you use lots of contracted forms, like 'don't' and 'can't'. Gestures, pauses and tone of voice all add to what you're saying too.

When you write, however, you use fewer contractions and punctuation marks tell you whether it's a question or an exclamation. Cool!

Pogo said that he was very hungry.

I'm starving!

Turn these written sentences into speech. Write your answers in the speech bubbles.

1 Twinx said that she loved Mini T.

2 Zen grumbled that he was very tired.

3 Nok shouted when he scored a goal.

4 Zara P said she would help.

5 Zing said that the song was excellent.

6 Pogo warned the aliens that he was coming.

7 The space-mobile driver shouted to the aliens to sit down.

8 The vet said that Zen needed to lose weight.

9 Twinx asked if Zara P would read her a story.

10 Nok said that he didn't understand his work.

11 Zen asked Nok to turn the music up.

12 Pogo shouted to try and wake up Zen.

13 Zara P shouted that she was going out.

14 Zen asked for a Z cookie.

15 The alien football referee sent the player off.

15 14 13 12 11 10 9 8 7 6 5 4 3 2 1

Easy! Have a musical sticker.

Colour in your score.

Main clauses

My notebook contains lots of complex sentences which contain more than one clause. The **main clause** gives us the key information and makes sense on its own. The subordinate clause adds more information.

My notebooks are full of information,

to help me learn.

main clause   subordinate clause

Commas help to separate the clauses, so your reader knows when to pause, and can understand what the sentence means. I'll just make a note of that …

Underline the main clause in each sentence.

1 Zen ate all his Z cookies, before falling asleep.

2 Scoring five goals, Nok's team won the football trophy.

3 Zing turned on his music player, to listen to some music.

4 Twinx played with Mini T, sitting on her bedroom floor.

5 Pogo bounced towards the space-mobile, leaving the other aliens behind.

6 Flying on her jet-scooter, Zara P can get about really quickly.

7 The aliens come from planet Dunk, in another galaxy.

8 The space-mobile took off, stirring up a cloud of dust.

9 Although the light was on, Zara P was not in her room.

10 Twinx was late, so she missed the space-mobile.

11 Pogo looked for Zen, finding him asleep in a crater.

12 Zara P couldn't put the book down, because it was so good.

13 Twinx practised her ballet, until it was perfect.

14 Zing always looks cool, even when he's asleep!

15 At the end of the football match, Nok was tired.

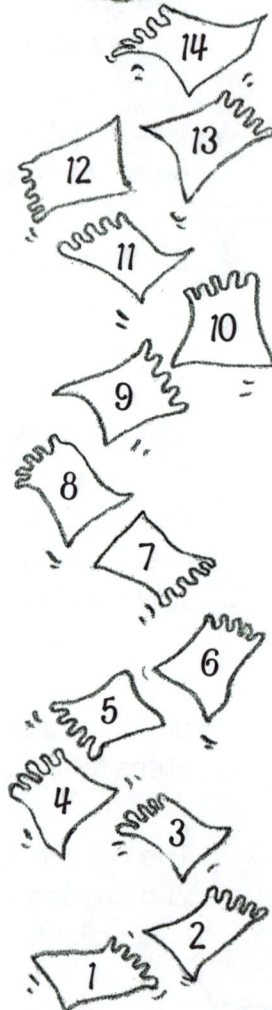

Zip, zip, zip! Have a scooter sticker.

Colour in your score.

Err, what? Spelling some words really tangles my antennae! They contain vowels that you can't hear clearly when you say the word.

For example, most people say 'factry', but it's spelt, factory.

With words like these, I suppose I just have to practise them until I remember where all the **unstressed vowels** go.

Write the correct spelling for each word in the goal.

1 busness

2 histry

3 intrest

4 listning

5 jewellry

6 happning

7 diffrence

8 refrence

9 frightning

10 genral

11 offring

12 mystry

13 seprate

14 boundry

15 dangrous

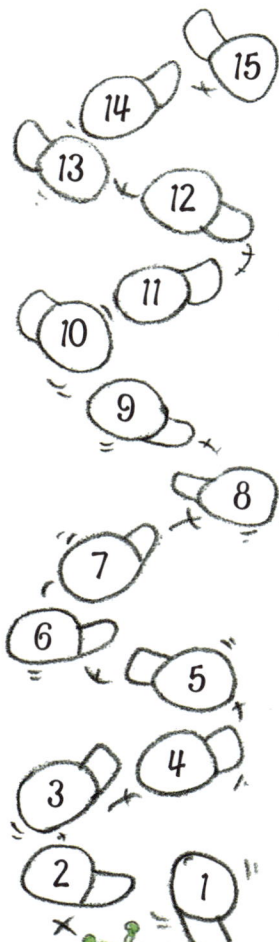

He shoots, he scores! Have a football sticker.

Colour in your score.

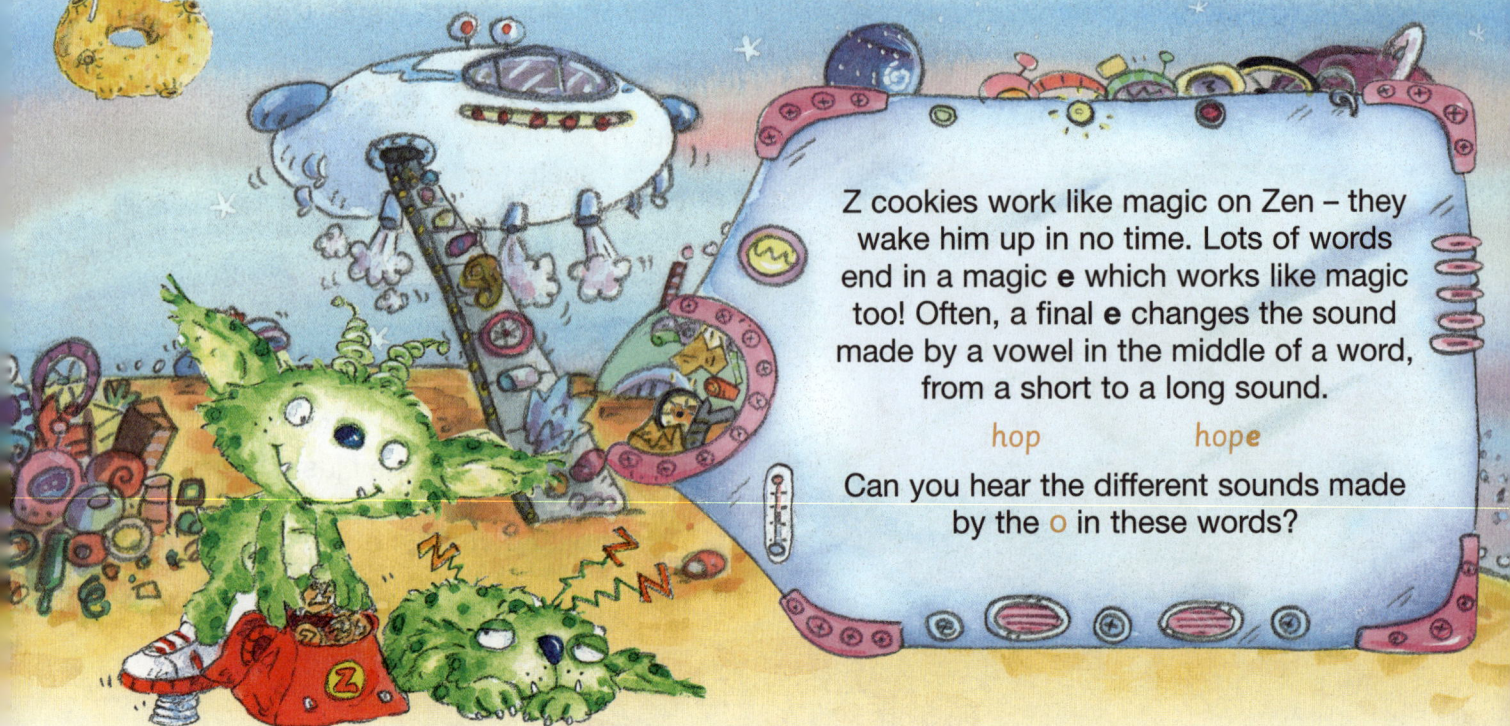

Z cookies work like magic on Zen – they wake him up in no time. Lots of words end in a magic **e** which works like magic too! Often, a final **e** changes the sound made by a vowel in the middle of a word, from a short to a long sound.

hop   hop**e**

Can you hear the different sounds made by the o in these words?

Some of these words should end in a modifying e and some should not. Add the e where you think you need to.

1 snak

2 rop

3 soap

4 trap

5 lak

6 fram

7 lip

8 tal

9 sock

10 light

11 pag

12 pil

13 road

14 dat

15 fit

15 14 13 12 11 10 9 8 7 6 5 4 3 2 1

Boing, boing, boing! Have a springy sticker.

Colour in your score.

Possessive apostrophes

Of all the things that belong to me, my Mini T and my radio are my favourites. We can use apostrophes to say when something belongs to a person or thing. That should keep my stuff safe!

For singular or collective nouns, the apostrophe goes before the **s**. For plural nouns, it goes after.

child**'s**   children**'s**   aliens**'**

There's one exception – its never has an apostrophe when you say something belongs to it! Oh dear, Mini T, this is a tricky one!

Add the apostrophes to these phrases, if you think they need one.

1 an aliens foot

2 Pogos trainers

3 the suns rays

4 the peoples homes

5 the mens cars

6 the cow flicked its tail

7 two mechanics tools

8 four space-mobiles docking bays

9 Zara Ps jet-scooter

10 three planets orbits

11 two cookies crumbs

12 Zings music

13 a dogs paws

14 planet Dunks atmosphere

15 nine boys boots

Hurray! Have a Mini T sticker.

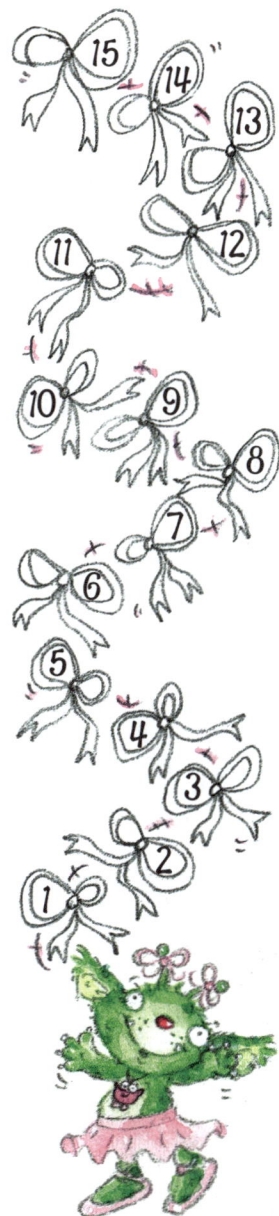

Colour in your score.

Look at Pogo bouncing about. He never stops! You can always tell where he's been, because his springs leave marks all over the place. Look in the space dust on the ground by that crater…

Prepositions like in, on and by are great, because they help us to describe where one thing is in relation to another. Relax – you can do this!

Pick a preposition from the cookie jar to complete these sentences, or choose one of your own.

1 Pogo bounced right _____ Zen.

2 Zen snuggled _____ the blanket and dozed off.

3 Twinx looked at her reflection _____ the mirror.

4 Pogo bought some more Z cookies _____ Zen.

5 Zing stores music _____ his music player.

6 Zara P zoomed _____ the night sky on her jet scooter.

7 The rocket shot _____ from Dunk.

8 Twinx keeps her Mini T _____ her neck.

9 The space-mobile was headed _____ Earth.

10 Nok kicked the ball straight _____ the goal.

11 The notebooks were written _____ Zara P.

12 Zen woke up _____ he smelt the Z cookies.

13 Zara P looked at Earth _____ her telescope.

14 Pogo stopped bouncing just _____ he knocked Twinx over.

15 Twinx hid _____ Zing.

through
before
into
behind
for
on
in
over
around
under
towards
across
away
by
after

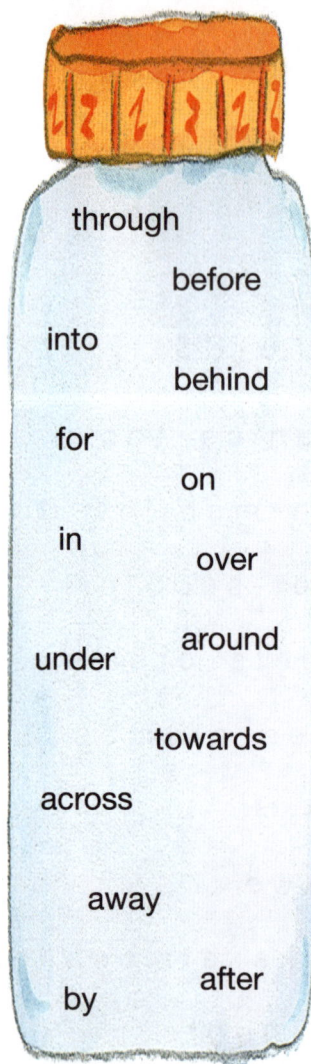

Good work! Have a Z cookie sticker.

Colour in your score.

I always used to write exactly the same, whoever my reader was. Then I learnt how to **adapt** my writing for different readers, by varying the words I use and the way I structure my sentences.

Now I can say something in a really formal way.

Henceforth I undertake to improve my performance.

Or I can say the same thing in an informal way.

Promise I'll do better next time!

Cool, huh?

Match these formal words and phrases with their less formal versions.

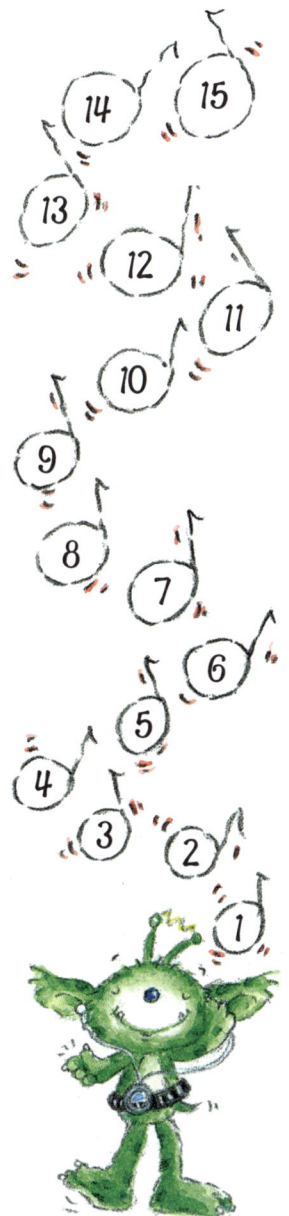

1	proceed directly to	A	wrong
2	located	B	you can pay by cheque
3	excessive quantity	C	arrested
4	misplaced	D	go straight to
5	henceforth	E	found
6	nevertheless	F	too much
7	purchase	G	imagine
8	disembark	H	not enough proof
9	cheques are acceptable	I	lost
10	consequently	J	even so
11	forbidden	K	buy
12	apprehended	L	not allowed
13	insufficient evidence	M	from now on
14	envisage	N	as a result
15	erroneous	O	get off

Easy! Have a musical sticker.

Colour in your score.

Suffixes

Zip, zip, zip! **Suffixes** are really zippy at changing words.

To add the suffixes es, ed or ness to a word which ends in a consonant and then y, you change the y to i first.

silly   silliness

You can add ing without changing the spelling, but if you want to add ly, you often have to change the y to i, but not always.

dry   drying

pretty   prettily

Let me just make a note of that …

Do these word sums.

1 fly + es = _____

2 tidy + ing = _____

3 shy + ly = _____

4 steady + es = _____

5 ready + ly = _____

6 bendy + ness = _____

7 friendly + ness = _____

8 rely + es = _____

9 worry + ing = _____

10 hurry + ed = _____

11 carry + ed = _____

12 floppy + ness = _____

13 happy + ly = _____

14 try + ed = _____

15 sly + ness = _____

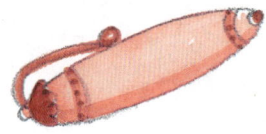

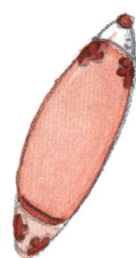

You're zippy! Have a scooter sticker.

Colour in your score.

Word formation

He shoots, he scores! Football matches move quickly, so I have to stay fit to keep up! The English language is changing all the time too and new words are always being made! Some are formed by **shortening** longer words.

of the clock
o'clock

Some come from removing **prefixes** or **suffixes**.

omnibus
bus

photograph
photo

Some are **acronyms**.

compact disc
CD

The words in the boots have all been formed from other words or phrases. Circle the correct origin for each one.

1	phone	telephone	phonetic
2	bike	bicycle	bikcyle
3	CD	compact drive	compact disc
4	pub	public toilet	public house
5	plane	skyplane	aeroplane
6	TV	television	televideo
7	WC	water cupboard	water closet
8	Halloween	Halloweven	All Hallow's Eve
9	UV	upper vault	ultraviolet
10	auto	autopilot	automatic
11	Xmas	Crossmas	Christmas
12	helipad	helicopter landing pad	helicopter seat pad
13	PG	parental guidance	public garden
14	movie	moving walkway	moving picture
15	DVD	digital video disc	diverting video disc

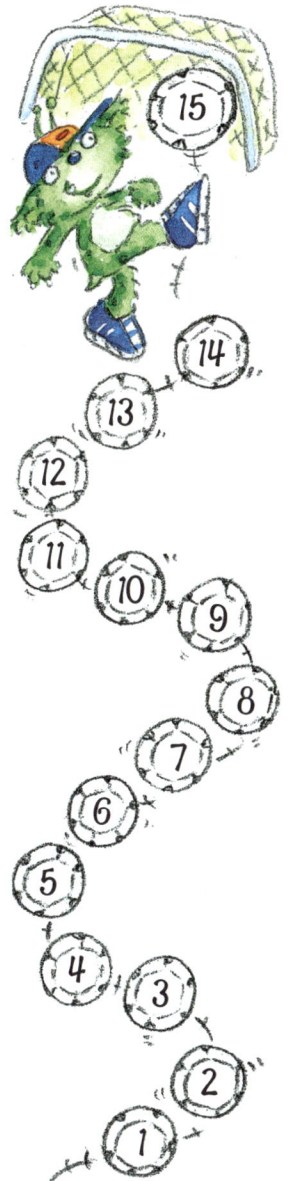

Goal! Have a football sticker.

Colour in your score.

Complex sentences are cool! They help to make your writing flow nicely. They have more than one clause – the main clause, which gives us the key information, and the subordinate clause, which adds extra information.

Sometimes, the subordinate clause is **embedded** within the sentence and we use commas to separate it from the rest of the sentence.

*The shooting star, **which was very bright**, lit up the whole sky.*

See? Easy!

Underline the embedded clause in these sentences.

1 Yesterday, after eating his tea, Nok played outside.

2 Zara P's jet scooter, with flames shooting out of the back, zoomed past.

3 Zen, who is Pogo's dog, is always sleeping.

4 Z cookies, kept in Pogo's rucksack, usually wake him up!

5 Tomorrow, because it is Saturday, Twinx is going to the cinema.

6 A parcel, sent from planet Earth, arrived for Zing.

7 The space-mobile, headed for Earth, took off into the sunset.

8 Zing's music, playing at full volume, could be heard next door.

9 Twinx's favourite toy, which is Mini T, goes everywhere with her.

10 Pogo bounced, without looking first, right into the puddle.

11 The comet, with its tail blazing, shot past planet Dunk.

12 Planet Dunk, where the aliens live, is in another galaxy.

13 The trip to planet Earth, as made by the space-mobile, takes only a few minutes.

14 Zara P's notebook, which she keeps in her bag, is full of useful information.

15 Zen, snoring loudly, rolled over in his sleep.

Easy! Have a musical sticker.

15 14 13 12 11 10 9 8 7 6 5 4 3 2 1

Colour in your score.

Letter strings

Oh no! I think I've picked up the wrong bag. It looks just like mine, but my notebook isn't in it...

My bag mix-up is a bit like some **letter strings**, which look the same, but make different sounds in different words.

4   *Flour*

four   *flour*

Let me just make a note of that... Oh no! I can't!

Join up the pairs of words in which the same letter strings make the same sound.

1 p**ear**

2 h**our**

3 p**our**

4 f**ear**

5 inst**ead**

6 b**ould**er

7 fl**ood**

8 b**ead**

though
shoulder
head
plead
would
bear
bough
sour
rough
hear
your
heat
learn
blood
threat

9 h**eard**

10 pl**ough**

11 d**ough**

12 tr**eat**

13 sw**eat**

14 c**ould**

15 en**ough**

15
14
13
12
11
10
9
8
7
6
5
4
3
2
1

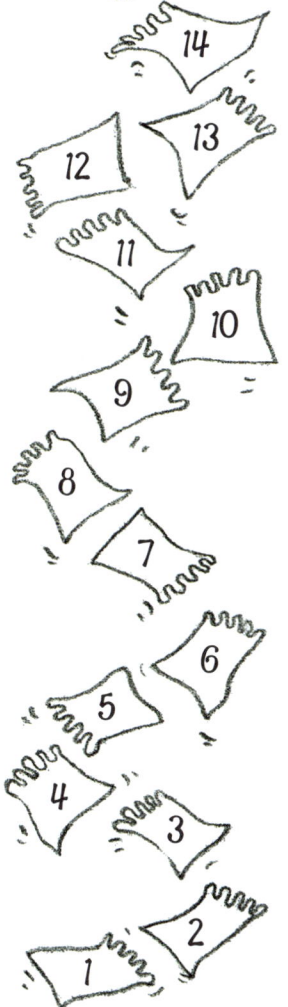

You're zippy! Have a scooter sticker.

Colour in your score.

Look at lazy old Zen, asleep again. One sniff of these Z cookies, though, and he'll be wide awake. He's such a pig!

When you describe something as if it were something else, it's called a **metaphor**. Great character descriptions are just a bounce away once you know how to use metaphors!

Ready, steady, bounce!

Draw lines to match up the metaphors with their meanings.

1	She's a bright spark.	He's really gentle.
2	He's the life and soul of the party.	He's having something tested on him.
3	You're a dark horse.	He's dependable.
4	She's a pain in the neck.	He doesn't fit in.
5	He's a wolf in sheep's clothing.	She has a rare talent.
6	He's a pussy cat.	You're a mystery.
7	He's a rock.	She's very famous.
8	She's a star.	He's unpredictable.
9	She's a rose between thorns.	He's really fun at parties.
10	It's the cat's whiskers.	She's not like the others in the family.
11	She's the black sheep of the family.	It's the very best.
12	He's a loose cannon.	She's very clever.
13	She's a treasure.	He's not to be trusted.
14	He's a square peg in a round hole.	She's annoying.
15	He's a guinea pig.	She's a pretty girl between two ugly people.

Put a spring in your step! Have a springy sticker.

Colour in your score.

Just like music and lyrics work together to make a great song, **nouns and verbs** have to work together when they appear in a sentence.

If the noun is singular, you have to use the singular verb form. If the noun is plural, you have to use the plural verb form.

she sings   they sing

Music to my ears!

Choose the correct verb from each set of headphones to complete these sentences.

1 The aliens _____ in the crater.
 plays / play

2 Pogo _____ on his springs.
 bounce / bounces

3 The stars _____ brightly.
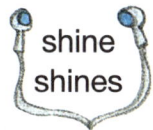 shine / shines

4 Twinx _____ in her bedroom.
 dances / dance

5 The Moon _____ full tonight.
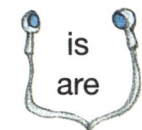 is / are

6 Pogo and Zen _____ planet Earth.
 visits / visit

7 A space-mobile _____ towards planet Dunk.
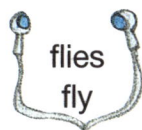 flies / fly

8 The craters _____ great places to play.
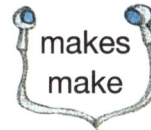 makes / make

9 Nok _____ a goal.
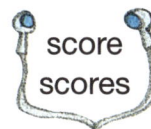 score / scores

10 Twinx _____ tired last night.
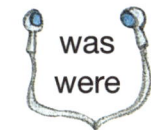 was / were

11 Zen _____ peacefully in his basket.
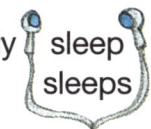 sleep / sleeps

12 Twinx _____ with her ribbons.
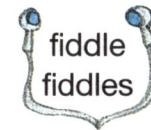 fiddle / fiddles

13 Planet Earth _____ tiny from planet Dunk.
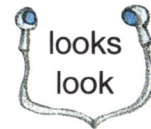 looks / look

14 The aliens _____ visiting planet Earth yesterday.
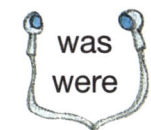 was / were

15 The mechanic _____ Zara P's jet scooter.
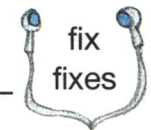 fix / fixes

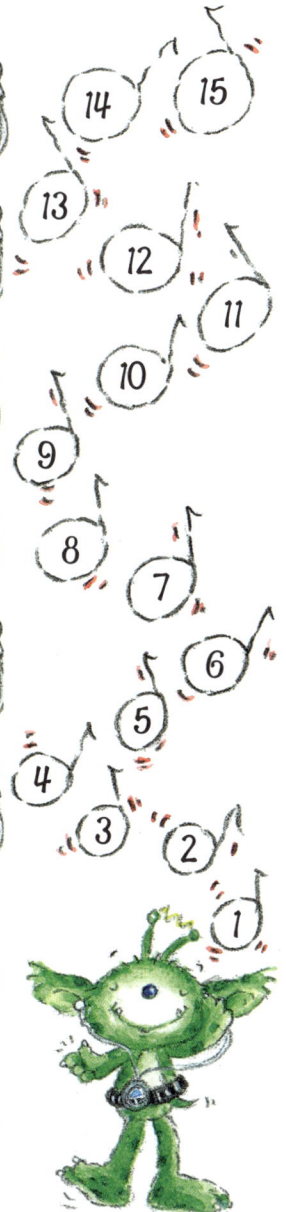

Congratulations! Have a last musical sticker for your certificate. Cool!

Colour in your score.

Answers

Test 1 Vowel endings
1 cameras
2 haloes or halos
3 cuckoos
4 radios
5 heroes
6 chapattis
7 tubas
8 zoos
9 areas
10 echoes
11 gnus
12 pianos
13 emus
14 bananas
15 tangos

Test 2 Plurals
Circled words should be:
1 planets
2 foxes
3 shoes
4 skies
5 bushes
6 torches
7 lorries
8 bees
9 ladies
10 eyes
11 buses
12 puppies
13 craters
14 studies
15 friends

Test 3 Prefixes
1 **bi**focal
2 **trans**mit
3 **circum**stance
4 **auto**matic
5 **auto**biography
6 **bi**noculars
7 **trans**late
8 **circum**navigate
9 **tele**scope
10 **bi**nary
11 **tele**vision
12 **circum**vent
13 **auto**pilot
14 **tele**pathy
15 **trans**fer

Test 4 Synonyms
Underlined words should be:
1 furious
2 hilarious
3 starving
4 saturated
5 freezing
6 ancient
7 ecstatic
8 boiling
9 sprint
10 hurl
11 miserable
12 dazzling
13 deafening
14 exhausted
15 shattered

Test 5 More prefixes
Circled words should be:
1 inactive
2 irrational
3 incredible
4 irregular
5 inconsiderate
6 irreversible
7 impure
8 indirect
9 irreplaceable
10 irrelevant
11 immature
12 imperfect
13 indecisive
14 impersonal
15 impolite

Test 6 Adverbs
Answers will vary, but the adverbs chosen should be appropriate to the verb and to the overall meaning of the sentence.

Test 7 Checking for mistakes
1 Remember not to be <u>lait</u> for the rocket launch.
2 Nok is filthy because he<u>,</u> has been playing football again.
3 Zing downloaded <u>has</u> more music.
4 The sunset was <u>imcredible</u> last night.
5 Zen was<u>,</u> asleep, so Pogo got out another Z cookie.
6 Twinx is practising her ballet<u> </u>
7 Nok has eaten four ice <u>lollys</u> today!
8 Pogo bounces all over the <u>plaice</u>.
9 <u>my</u> jet scooter needs a good clean.
10 Twinx <u>playing</u> is with Mini T.
11 Look how <u>brite</u> that star is!
12 <u>the</u> fleet of space ships has landed.
13 'Hell<u>a</u>!' said Twinx.
14 Zing loves to <u>cool</u> look.
15 Zen is always sleeping<u> </u>

Test 8 Direct and reported speech
1 D
2 D
3 R
4 D
5 R
6 R
7 D
8 D
9 R
10 R
11 D
12 D
13 R
14 D
15 R

Test 9 Nouns

Common nouns	Abstract nouns	Proper nouns
planet	anger	Earth
crater	knowledge	Friday
rocket	confusion	Zen
scooter	happiness	January
comet	hatred	Twinx

Test 10 Imperative verbs
1 <u>Locate</u> your springy trainers.
2 <u>Put</u> them on.
3 <u>Bounce</u> down to the shop.
4 <u>Choose</u> the biggest box of Z cookies in the shop.
5 <u>Take out</u> your money.
6 <u>Pay</u> for the cookies.
7 <u>Wait</u> for your change.
8 <u>Bring</u> the cookies back home.
9 <u>Find</u> a very large bowl.
10 <u>Fill</u> it to the brim.
11 <u>Place</u> the bowl on the floor beside me.
12 <u>Refill</u> it when I have finished.
13 <u>Clear</u> up the crumbs on the floor.
14 <u>Fetch</u> me a cushion.
15 <u>Leave</u> me in peace, for a nap!

Test 11 Idioms
1 **N**
2 **O**
3 **I**
4 **K**
5 **J**
6 **E**
7 **L**
8 **M**
9 **B**
10 **F**
11 **D**
12 **A**
13 **G**
14 **C**
15 **H**

Test 12 Homophones
Circled words should be:
1 waste
2 sun
3 buy
4 allowed
5 ate
6 threw
7 night
8 tale
9 wait
10 floor
11 for
12 bear
13 brakes
14 bread
15 needs

Test 13 Adding ing
1 taking
2 going
3 flying
4 running
5 writing
6 travelling
7 leaving
8 eating
9 dreaming
10 believing
11 winning
12 reading
13 sitting
14 getting
15 living

Test 14 Antonyms

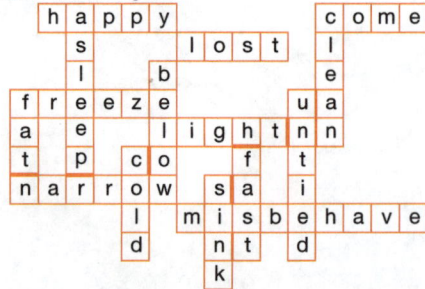

(crossword grid)
happy / come / sl / lost / l / e / b / e / freeze / ua / ae / e / light / nn / tp / co / ft / ti / narrow / sai / l / misbehave / d / nt / k

Test 15 Onomatopeia
Answers may vary, but might include:
1 splash
2 drip
3 plop
4 smash
5 splinter
6 crash
7 bang
8 whoosh
9 pop
10 tweet
11 squawk
12 chirrup
13 wail
14 howl
15 scream

Test 16 Spoken and written English
Answers will vary, but might include:
1 I love Mini T!
2 I'm very tired!
3 Goal!
4 I'll help.
5 This song's great!
6 Look out!
7 Sit down!
8 You're too fat, Zen.
9 Please read to me.
10 I don't get this!
11 Turn the music up.
12 Wake up!
13 I'm off out!
14 Can I have a cookie?
15 That's it! You're off!

Test 17 Main clauses
1 <u>Zen ate all his Z cookies</u>, before falling asleep.
2 Scoring five goals, <u>Nok's team won the football trophy</u>.
3 <u>Zing turned on his music player</u>, to listen to some music.
4 <u>Twinx played with Mini T</u>, sitting on her bedroom floor.
5 <u>Pogo bounced towards the space-mobile</u>, leaving the other aliens behind.
6 Flying on her jet-scooter, <u>Zara P can get about really quickly</u>.
7 <u>The aliens come from planet Dunk</u>, in another galaxy.
8 <u>The space-mobile took off</u>, stirring up a cloud of dust.
9 Although the light was on, <u>Zara P was not in her room</u>.
10 <u>Twinx was late</u>, so she missed the space-mobile.
11 <u>Pogo looked for Zen</u>, finding him asleep in a crater.
12 <u>Zara P couldn't put the book down</u>, because it was so good.
13 <u>Twinx practised her ballet</u>, until it was perfect.
14 <u>Zing always looks cool</u>, even when he's asleep!
15 At the end of the football match, <u>Nok was tired</u>.

Test 18 Unstressed vowels
1 business
2 history
3 interest
4 listening
5 jewellery
6 happening
7 difference
8 reference
9 frightening
10 general
11 offering
12 mystery
13 separate
14 boundary
15 dangerous

Test 19 Modifying e
1 snake
2 rope
3 soap
4 trap
5 lake
6 frame
7 lip
8 tale
9 sock
10 light
11 page
12 pile
13 road
14 date
15 fit

Test 20 Possessive apostrophes
1 an alien's foot
2 Pogo's trainers
3 the sun's rays
4 the people's homes
5 the men's cars
6 the cow flicked its tail
7 two mechanics' tools
8 four space-mobiles' docking bays
9 Zara P's jet scooter
10 three planets' orbits
11 two cookies' crumbs
12 Zing's music
13 a dog's paws
14 Dunk's atmosphere
15 nine boys' boots

Test 21 Prepositions
Answers may vary, but possible answers are:
1 Pogo bounced right **over** Zen.
2 Zen snuggled **under** the blanket and dozed off.
3 Twinx looked at her reflection **in** the mirror.
4 Pogo bought some more Z cookies **for** Zen.
5 Zing stores music **on** his music player.
6 Zara P zoomed **across** the night sky on her jet scooter.
7 The rocket shot **away** from Dunk.
8 Twinx keeps her Mini T **around** her neck.
9 The space-mobile was headed **towards** Earth.
10 Nok kicked the ball straight **into** the goal.
11 The notebooks were written **by** Zara P.
12 Zen woke up **after** he smelt the Z cookies.
13 Zara P looked at Earth **through** her telescope.
14 Pogo stopped bouncing just **before** he knocked Twinx over.
15 Twinx hid **behind** Zing.

Test 22 Adapting text
1 D
2 E
3 F
4 I
5 M
6 J
7 K
8 O
9 B
10 N
11 L
12 C
13 H
14 G
15 A

Test 23 Suffixes
1 flies
2 tidying
3 shyly
4 steadies
5 readily
6 bendiness
7 friendliness
8 relies
9 worrying
10 hurried
11 carried
12 floppiness
13 happily
14 tried
15 slyness

Test 24 Word formation
The circled words should be:
1 telephone
2 bicycle
3 compact disc
4 public house
5 aeroplane
6 television
7 water closet
8 All Hallow's Eve
9 ultraviolet
10 automatic
11 Christmas
12 helicopter landing pad
13 parental guidance
14 moving picture
15 digital video disc

Test 25 Embedded clauses
1 Yesterday, after eating his tea, Nok played outside.
2 Zara P's jet scooter, with flames shooting out of the back, zoomed past.
3 Zen, who is Pogo's dog, is always sleeping.
4 Z cookies, kept in Pogo's rucksack, usually wake him up!
5 Tomorrow, because it is Saturday, Twinx is going to the cinema.
6 A parcel, sent from planet Earth, arrived for Zing.
7 The space-mobile, headed for Earth, took off into the sunset.
8 Zing's music, playing at full volume, could be heard next door.
9 Twinx's favourite toy, which is Mini T, goes everywhere with her.
10 Pogo bounced, without looking first, right into the puddle.
11 The comet, with its tail blazing, shot past planet Dunk.
12 Planet Dunk, where the aliens live, is in another galaxy.
13 The trip to planet Earth, as made by the space-mobile, takes only a few minutes.
14 Zara P's notebook, which she keeps in her bag, is full of useful information.
15 Zen, snoring loudly, rolled over in his sleep.

Test 26 Letter strings
1 pear → bear
2 hour → sour
3 pour → your
4 fear → hear
5 instead → head
6 boulder → shoulder
7 flood → blood
8 bead → plead
9 heard → learn
10 plough → bough
11 dough → though
12 treat → heat
13 sweat → threat
14 could → would
15 enough → rough

Test 27 Metaphors
1 She's very clever.
2 He's really fun at parties.
3 You're a mystery.
4 She's annoying.
5 He's not to be trusted.
6 He's really gentle.
7 He's dependable.
8 She's very famous.
9 She's a pretty girl between two ugly people.
10 It's the very best.
11 She's not like the others in the family.
12 He's unpredictable.
13 She has a rare talent.
14 He doesn't fit in.
15 He's having something tested on him.

Test 28 Nouns and verbs
The correct words are:
1 play
2 bounces
3 shine
4 dances
5 is
6 visit
7 flies
8 make
9 scores
10 was
11 sleeps
12 fiddles
13 looks
14 were
15 fixes

Alien Club Certificate

Congratulations, _____, from everyone on planet Dunk!
You have collected all your award stickers and are now a member of the
English 9-10 Alien Club.
You are out of this world!